The Dogs the Tree and the Hill

By Andy Keith

To My Wife, Kids and Dogs for Their Love and Support. Thank you for showing me we can do hard things.

Published In Loving Memory of Henry and Gracie

King Henry and Princess Grace

Preface

First there was Bootsie then Pepi, then Sam then Suzy then Henry then Gracie, now Tyler, Emma and Tucker. So blessed by the dogs who have raised me. My life has always been filled with copious amounts of mad dog love. Living with a dog or as part of a pack is how I choose to live.

Being responsible. Being able to respond. Being Response Able takes practice. Caring for another, caring for a dog is a huge responsibility. You are responsible for feeding and walking and cleaning-up every mess they make. Until it becomes an expression of love it will be hard work. Throughout my dog mastering experience the dog gives way more care feeding and love to his forever friend than the master to his dog. I believe a human is incapable of giving love so completely like a dog. The intensity of their love is hard to articulate. My daughter said the other day when her mother bemoaned the short life of dogs, "It's just them dog years momma…" Dogs are living life seven times faster than us. "The candle that burns twice as bright burns half as long." Blade Runner.

I hope you enjoy this glimpse into my wonderful life with dogs.

Chapter 1

The Dogs the Tree and the Hill

These are my dogs; Tyler, Emma and Tucker. We take long walks together. Our two favorite walks are to the Tree and to the Hill. When we go to the Tree or to the Hill we help each other find their place in this family. We help each other find our place in the world.

This is the Tree.

This is the Hill.

+Chapter 2

The Dogs

    Tyler is a very special boy. He is a rescue dog. He was homeless for the first two years of his life. When he first joined our family he had a lot of problems. He was missing a toe and he was very angry. Back then we still had Princess Grace and she was able to show him what to do. She was very old, but also very tough. He loved her very much.

They played really rough and Gracie was able to show him his place in the family. She helped Tyler find his place in the world. When Gracie got cancer Tyler became very gentle with her. When she died he was very sad. When Emma came into our lives Tyler knew just what to do.

She was a beautiful puppy golden doodle! She was so afraid of Tyler the first time she met him. She ran away crying, but he is such a good big brother. Tyler loved Emma from the first moment he saw her. She's so smart. She grew so fast and was able to give her older brother a run for his money.

Emma has become quite famous. You can find her at #emmathedood on Instagram. You can follow me on Instagram too at #keythink.

Emma is an incredible athlete. She runs up and down Western Colorado mountains like their East Coast hills. Emma is quite possibly the fastest dog ever.

Emma very easily found her place in our family and she helps us all to find our place in the world.

When Tucker came into our lives he was sort of a little guy, but what he lacked in size he made up for with enthusiasm!

Tyler did not stay little for long.

Tucker loves Emma. She helps him know his place in the world. Tucker thinks he may be the fastest dog ever.

Tucker loves to go to the Hill.

The dogs love the Hill.

This is the view from the top of the Hill. On this day there was a cloud in front of Mount Garfield but I took the shot anyways I love the vail of cloud mist Taking pictures at the top of the Hill with the dogs has helped me find my place in the world. Some of my pictures from the top of the Hill received some praise from family and friends. My mother-in-law said I could print them, and frame them and that I should be a real photographer. Like her daughter she is always right. No, seriously. So I printed one and framed it.

Chapter 3

The Tree

We can walk to the tree from our house so we get to go there often. It sits out next to a huge corn field and creek.

Tyler, Emma and Tucker love the shade under the Tree! Tucker loves it so much he kicks up dust.

View from the Hill

View from the Hill

Emma is the King of the Hill! On this walk we pushed it a little further and I think we may have found a new hill. About a mile NorthWest from here lies Hill 2.0

Sometimes coming back down the Hill is the best part. The sunsets are spectacular.

My wife told me to post some of my pictures and I thought she said take some pictures of posts. You can find me and links to my blogs at **andykeith.com**

Suzy likes walking to the Tree too! Her mom told me I should put my pictures in a book. Suzy, the Girls, the Dogs, the Hill and the Tree help me know my place in the world. Every day they show me that we can do hard things.

Love always, Andy Keith, CEO William Penrose Publishing

The End